Draw Near

DRAW NEAR

AN ADVENT DEVOTIONAL

LAURA PYNE

Draw Near: An Advent Devotional
By Laura A. Pyne

Copyright © 2019 by Laura A. Pyne

Cover design: Laura A. Pyne
Interior design: Benjamin Vrbicek (benjaminvrbicek.com)

Trade paperback ISBN: 9781096432395

For my parents, who chose me first,
loved me first, and pointed me to God first and always.
I love you, Mom and Dad.

Table of Contents

Introduction

I DON'T KNOW YOU. I don't know your story. I don't know your hurts. I don't know your dreams.

To be honest, there's a lot I don't know.

But, there's also something I *do* know.

I know that sometime around 2000 years ago, a Savior was sent into our world in the form of a tiny baby. Since then? *Everything* changed.

These days, the Christmas season—the time we celebrate the birth of that tiny baby and look with hope toward the return of our King—often takes on a different tone than in ages past.

Between the parties, the gift buying, the rush that seems to start earlier and earlier, and, the preparations that each of these entails, the season is filled with more and more busyness and fewer and fewer chances to simply breathe, let alone focus on what matters most.

I believe we're called to do better. I believe we are called to prepare our hearts and our whole selves during the Advent season. I believe we are called to *draw near.*

Before you start to worry about squeezing something else into your schedule, I'd like to ask you to step back for a minute or two... to start at the beginning to understand what I mean by 'draw near.'

An "advent" is the arrival of a notable person, thing or event. To believers, the Advent season is meant to help us prepare for and celebrate the arrival of Jesus Christ on that night that changed the course of history, providing us access to a personal relationship with our God. It's also meant to help us prepare for his second coming, to the Advent season that lasts all year, providing us with a future hope.

Unfortunately, much of this significance gets lost in the busyness our culture imposes on us during this time of year. How can we find room to prepare for something else?

I have good news!

In the Bible, in James 4:8, we are promised if we *draw near to God, he will draw near to us.*

Even better—perhaps—in Psalm 145:18, we're reminded that "The LORD is near to all who call on him, to all who call on him in truth."

You see, for those of us who believe in God the Father, in his Son, in his resurrection and the promise it brings, God is already near.

Far too often, we turn our relationship with God into a chore, into a list of 'to-dos' that matches other tasks in our lives. It doesn't need to be this way. In fact, it *shouldn't* be this way at all.

God requires all of us. Our devotion. Our hearts. Our hopes. Our dreams. But, he has already equipped us for the task, leaving us with a simple challenge: draw near.

I'd like to challenge you to keep this in mind as you read and work through this devotional and, more importantly, through this Advent season.

While each day will include a journal prompt, at the root of each is a simple challenge: open your heart, focus on the true meaning of the season, and draw near to the one who knows the stars and calls them by name. The one who has already come. The one who will come again. The one who is already waiting, drawing you nearer to him.

Turn Around

*I will give them a heart to know that I am the L*ORD*, and they shall be my people and I will be their God, for they shall return to me with their whole heart.*

Jeremiah 24:7

*"And a Redeemer will come to Zion, to those in Jacob who turn from transgression," declares the L*ORD*.*

Isaiah 59:20

Return O faithless sons; I will heal your faithlessness.

Jeremiah 3:22a

BEFORE WE GO ANY FARTHER ON THIS JOURNEY—into more scripture and more study—do you need to turn around?

Turn around?

I never knew such a simple idea could be so radical.

You see, I grew up in a Christian home. I knew scripture by heart. I believed in God. But, like many of us, I also wanted to enjoy high school, college, "real life" and everything that went along with it. I felt the burden of my actions with strong convictions, but I held them at bay. I didn't want to do the fixing. That could wait for later, *after* the fun.

Then one night, my then boyfriend, now husband, and I went to a concert put on by a big name in the Christian music world. What this artist shared changed both of our lives.

"God wants you to turn around," he said. "You don't need to fix anything. Turn around. Invite him in. He will help you through the rest."

So simple. So radically necessary.

I'd been putting off the heart-changing "work," because it felt bigger than me... but, how could I "get right" with God without it?

I needed to turn around. I'd forgotten the simple truth that when we draw near to God, he draws near to us. We don't need to fix things *then* turn around and walk toward our Lord. We need to turn around. He meets us exactly where we are. That's when the heart fixing can begin, with him before us, behind us and beside us.

As we journey into Advent, right now, at the start, God is calling us to turn around. Not to fix everything first, but to simply come.

That request doesn't come without a promise, a promise relevant now and always: God promises that when we come to him, he will give us a heart to know him. He will heal our faithlessness. He will—and did—send a redeemer!

When we sincerely turn to him, he will change our hearts, our desires, and our needs to align with his heart and his plan for our lives.

Will it hurt? Yes. Will it require change? Yes. But, the challenge we face is not to bear these changes alone, our challenge is to turn around.

As you embark on this Advent journey, is God calling you to turn to him? Have you been avoiding that call, or making it harder than it needs to be? There's never been a better time. Your Savior awaits; seek him first.

Journal

What areas of your life have you been holding on to, rather than giving them to God? Write them down, then, ask him to meet you in those places. Ask him for a heart like his.

_____

_____

_____

_____

_____

_____

_____

_____

_____

_____

_____

_____

_____

Find Joy for the Journey

*Serve the LORD with gladness! Come into his presence with sing-
ing! Know that the LORD, he is God! It is he who made us, and we
are his; we are his people, and the sheep of his pasture. Enter
his gates with thanksgiving, and his courts with praise! Give
thanks to him; bless his name!*

Psalm 100:2–4

WHILE DIFFERENT TERMS AND WORDS ARE USED IN various translations of the Bible, one of the most dominant themes—regardless of translation—is *joy*. God desires our joy.

Before moving forward, I think it's important to separate God's vision of joy from the "happiness" this world has taught us to chase above all else, has taught us we "deserve."

Not satisfied in your relationship—even your marriage? *Find someone new.*

Working hard in a job you hate? *You deserve better.*

Not content to live out "ancient" or "dated" Biblical de-mands? *You do you.*

Our notion of the holiday season often gets God's desire for joy crossed with the happiness we so often find ourselves chasing.

Now's a great time to rewind.

An excellent starting point is the book of Psalms, the book that illustrates the depths of despair, intertwined with true joy. It provides a full picture of the cycle so many of us find ourselves in regularly.

Life is hard. It hurts. You've experienced pain that is so real you can feel it. Despair that makes waking up a challenge. Unanswered questions that permeate you to the core. Loss. Illness. Impossible financial hurdles. The list could go on and on.

When we are in the middle of times like those, joy feels like a joke. In God's design, however, maybe it shouldn't.

Our joy is not meant to come from this world. Though we might catch glimpses of it from time to time, that expectation might be what leads to our misplaced, discombobulated idea of joy.

Reflect on Psalm 100:2–4 again.

Our joy? It wasn't supposed to be this-life-based. It is to come from and rest in our creator. The one who draws us to himself, who shepherds us and who calls us his own.

Our joy should come from our identity in Christ and the promise he fulfilled when he sent his son to our world to begin a journey to the cross, designed to bridge the gap that this world—"happiness" and all—made so wide.

This world will continue to hurt, to cause despair. This season, let's look for the joy that can only be found in God. Joy that is far from situational. Joy meant to sustain us though this journey of life.

Journal

How does God's idea of joy differ from your own? In what ways have you been chasing happiness that doesn't align with God's design? How can you practice and hold on to his joy this Advent season?

Reflect and Trust:
Something Great is in Store

The book of the genealogy of Jesus Christ, the son of David, the son of Abraham.

Abraham was the father of Isaac, and Isaac the father of Jacob, and Jacob the father of Judah and his brothers, and Judah the father of Perez and Zerah by Tamar, and Perez the father of Hezron, and Hezron the father of Ram and Ram the father of Amminadab, and Amminadab the father of Nahshon, and Nahshon the father of Salmon, and Salmon the father of Boaz by Rahab, and Boaz the father of Obed by Ruth, and Obed the father of Jesse, and Jesse the father of David the king.

And David was the father of Solomon by the wife of Uriah, and Solomon the father of Rehoboam, and Rehoboam the father of Abijah, and Abijah the father of Asaph, and Asaph the father of Jehoshaphat, and Jehoshaphat the father of Joram, and Joram the father of Uzziah, and Uzziah the father of Jotham, and Jotham the father of Ahaz, and Ahaz the father of Hezekiah, and Hezekiah the father of Manasseh, and Manasseh the father of Amos, and Amos the father of Josiah,and Josiah the father of Jechoniah and his brothers, at the time of the deportation to Babylon.

And after the deportation to Babylon: Jechoniah was the father of Shealtiel, and Shealtiel the father of Zerubbabel, and Zerubbabel the father of Abiud, and Abiud the father of Eliakim, and Eliakim the father of Azor, and Azor the father of Zadok, and Zadok the father of Achim, and Achim the father of Eliud, and Eliud the father of Eleazar, and Eleazar the father of Matthan, and Matthan the father of Jacob, and Jacob the father of Joseph the husband of Mary, of whom Jesus was born, who is called Christ.

So all the generations from Abraham to David were fourteen generations, and from David to the deportation to Babylon fourteen generations, and from the deportation to Babylon to the Christ fourteen generations.

Matthew 1:1–17

BIBLICAL STORIES, stories of the underdog, of God's power and might, of life lessons that still very much apply to our lives today and of God leading his people in ways greater than we could ever imagine... are exciting.

Today's passage, at first glance, might seem, well, less than exciting. But, that's not the reality at all.

It's easy to glaze over chapters and books that review numbers, specifications and lineages. By diving into this series of verses in Matthew, however, we should be excited. Especially as we march toward the fulfillment of this line.

This line, forty-two generations long, is more than a historical record. It is documented proof that our heavenly father planned the most perfect way to bring his son into the world and saw that plan through—over centuries—to ensure each and every piece was just right.

The players in this story are far from ordinary. They had no clue that they were part of something so much bigger than themselves. They lived entire lives without seeing or understanding how God's plan would unfold, in spite of their actions.

Think about them. Their waiting, their struggles, their sins. Abraham was 100 years old when his son, Isaac, was born, despite having been promised descendants that would be like the stars.

Isaac was nearly sacrificed on an altar by his father, until God provided a lamb.

Judah slept with a woman disguised as a prostitute, engaged to marry his son.

Solomon's mother was married to King David, who had ordered her husband murdered to cover their affair.

Jeconiah was king of Judah, dethroned by Babylon and taken into captivity.

Mary faced possible execution for becoming pregnant out of wedlock while engaged to Jesus's earthly father.

This cast of characters was far from perfect. Many experienced hardships we cannot fathom—exile, threat of death, waiting in agony and more. Yet, God's plan, his perfect, eternal plan—was fulfilled through each of them.

As you reflect on this, a theme becomes apparent: God has a plan, and that plan *will* be fulfilled above all else.

This is just as true for us today as it was in Jesus's time. We are used to instant gratification and building the lives we are told we deserve. Yet, these efforts require little trust and are often filled with disappointment.

God's plan, however, requires trust. It sometimes means pain. It requires us to take paths that might not make any sense to us or to those around us.

But, when *he* is leading the way and we are spending time in his Word while trusting fully in the fact that this God who loves us is working to bring about the best plan—his plan—then the waiting, the hurting and the questioning serve a greater purpose. This is true even if we don't get to see it come to fruition on this side of heaven.

Are you trusting fully in God's plan this Advent season?

Journal

Think back and jot down the times in your life that you felt God's leading. Struggling? That's okay. Think about situations that played out in a way you knew wasn't your own doing. Are you able to reflect on these circumstances to fully trust in God's plan for your life? Where is there room for your trust to grow?

Prepare the Way for the Lord

Comfort, comfort my people, says your God. Speak tenderly to Jerusalem, and cry to her that her warfare is ended, that her iniquity is pardoned, that she has received from the LORD's hand double for all her sins. A voice cries: "In the wilderness prepare the way of the Lord; make straight in the desert a highway for our God. Every valley shall be lifted up, and every mountain and hill be made low; the uneven ground shall become level, and the rough places a plain. And the glory of the LORD shall be revealed, and all flesh shall see it together, for the mouth of the LORD has spoken."

Isaiah 40:1–5

He said, "I am the voice of the one crying out in the wilderness, 'Make straight the way of the Lord.' As the prophet Isaiah said."

John 1:23

WHEN SOMETHING BIG HAPPENS IN THE BIBLE, God often prepares his people for it, whether they're aware of it or not.

Much of the Old Testament is exactly that: the story of God preparing his people and the world for the arrival of his son, who would ultimately fulfill many prophecies, covenants and promises.

In Isaiah, a voice of one calling in the desert "prepare the way for the Lord," whom John the Baptist later identifies himself as (John 1:23), is referenced.

God, through his prophet, is preparing his people for what's to come, offering comfort and hope, yet, demanding a certain level of repentance from sin as preparation for his Son's arrival.

God is offering glimpses of what's to come and providing hope, but requiring effort as well.

Today, Jesus *has* come. But, as we prepare to celebrate that coming and await the fulfillment of other promises found in scripture and offered to those who place their faith in Christ, that effort is also required of us.

God demands all of us. He wants his followers to be on fire for him, prepared for his calling, ready to lay it on the line for him at all times.

But, it's hard to be on fire for something—anything—if we're holding on to anything that douses that flame.

God is perfect in a way none of us can truly grasp. He is completely separate from sin. Does that mean we must be perfect as well?

No. We cannot be. The reason Jesus was sent in the first place was to be the *only* blemish-less sacrifice for our sin, the *only* acceptable offering.

That doesn't give us a free pass. We are called to abide by God's standards and to repent—turn away—from sin in our lives. If we are knowingly holding on to that sin, whatever it might be... a lie, a habit, anger, hatred, jealousy... we cannot be fully prepared for God's good and glorious plans in our lives.

Advent is a time of preparation, a time to repent, to draw nearer to God. He promises to fulfil the plans he has for our lives—something he could do without us—but, wouldn't it be best to be prepared?

Journal

What sin are you holding on to today? What "wilderness" lives in your heart that you could give to God to prepare for his plans in your life?

_____

_____

_____

_____

_____

_____

_____

_____

_____

_____

_____

_____

_____

Tune Out the Noise to Find Rest

Be still, and know that I am God. I will be exalted among the
nations, I will be exalted in the earth!

Psalm 46:10

But when you pray, go into your room and shut the door and
pray to your Father who is in secret. And your Father who sees
in secret will reward you.

Matthew 6:6

For God alone my soul waits in silence; from him comes my sal-
vation.

Psalm 62:1

WHEN'S THE LAST TIME YOU EXPERIENCED TRUE *QUIET*?
Regardless of your situation, whether you have
five kids, a busy career, a booming social life, an
innate need to be on the go, or, a little bit of all of these and
more, "quiet" is probably not a word you'd use to describe
many aspects of your life.

This is compounded even more by the conveniences we're
all "blessed" with today: social media, smart phones, wireless
home systems that pump music and information into every

room of our homes, the need to be available around the clock and more.

Don't get me wrong, there's a lot to enjoy when it comes to modern technology and advances, but, they make it awfully easy to neglect quiet.

You've probably felt the pressure that builds when peace is hard to find. To combat it, perhaps you spend time in nature, book time at a spa, hit the road for a run or curl up in your favorite reading nook. I know these are all part of my "stress relief" plan.

But, maybe those places and activities shouldn't be the first places we run.

Today's verses make it clear that God desires us to be still, to be quiet. To experience real, authentic "rest," we must be willing to tune out the noise that constantly surrounds us, preparing him room to lead us and work in our hearts and lives. We must intentionally quiet our hearts to listen.

Unfortunately, that's not natural to us.

I don't think that's a coincidence. We are accustomed to and surrounded by noise by another's design, by the design that is in place to separate us from the only one we will every truly need.

Let's break the pattern. Let's use this season of reflecting and waiting to do it well. Let's focus on spending time with the only one who can bring restoration, peace and satisfaction to our lives.

How can you draw near to God by finding quiet, away from the noise of everyday life?

Journal

Make a plan. List the ways you currently seek rest. In what way could time with God become a part of, or even replace, some of these? Ask God to quiet your heart and to provide you with true rest, today.

_____

_____

_____

_____

_____

_____

_____

_____

_____

_____

_____

_____

_____

Receive the Grace:
A Willing Heart

The true light, which gives light to everyone, was coming into the world. He was in the world, and the world was made through him, yet the world did not know him. He came to his own, and his own people did not receive him. But to all who did receive him, who believe in his name, he gave the right to become children of God, who were born, not of blood nor of the will of the flesh nor of the will of man, but of God.

And the Word became flesh and dwelt among us, and we have seen his glory, glory as of the only Son from the Father, full of grace and truth. (John bore witness about him, and cried out, "This was he of whom I said, 'He who comes after me ranks before me, because he was before me.'") For from his fullness we have all received grace upon grace. For the law was given through Moses; grace and truth came through Jesus Christ. No one has ever seen God; the only God, who is at the Father's side, he has made him known.

John 1:9–18

WE HAVE AN ADVANTAGE THAT THOSE LIVING UNDER THE law at the time of Jesus's birth didn't have; the opportunity to understand—at least grasp—and live in grace.

So... do we do it?

For those who've grown up in the church, I think the concept can be even more challenging to grasp. This has been my experience and has come up in conversations with many Christian friends.

Many of us have never struggled to accept the circumstances surrounding Jesus's birth. We believe his teachings. We understand the fact that God loves us and desires a relationship with us. But then, something happens.

We start to frame the relationship we have with God, made possible by the birth, death and resurrection of his Son, in human terms. Perhaps it's because of our single-framed, human comprehension, but maybe it's something else: a failure to understand God's unique, completely unhuman, grace.

We fall short, regardless of our efforts to follow God's commands and teaching, and we assume—incorrectly—that God's love for us becomes less. Are there consequences for our sins? Yes. The Bible (Romans 6:23) tells us that the "wages of sin is death, BUT" (and this is a big one, THE big one) "the gift of God is eternal life in Christ Jesus our Lord."

All of this is made possible by, you guessed it: grace.

On our own, we deserve nothing. Our very being makes us completely separate from the holiness of God. But, through a grace that can only come from a loving God, if we've placed our hearts and trust in him, that gaping chasm is closed.

We are his today and tomorrow. In our successes and failures. In our following and in our falling short. By grace, and the receiving of his light, sent out to our world two millennia ago, we were given the "right to become children of God," as John 1:9–18 details.

We had the law through Moses, God's expectations and commands. But, the grace now offered to us, came only through God's own Son.

Our role in this? To admit our inability to meet God's perfect, infallible standard on our own, and, to have willing and contrite hearts, ready to accept and receive the grace that is now—following great sacrifice—so freely given.

Is your heart willing to accept God's perfect grace this Advent season? Are you drawing near to God by accepting his grace, sent to you through his Son?

Journal

What does "grace" mean to you? How does it differ from God's grace? How does God's sending of Jesus change your view of grace? How can you personalize that, today?

_____

_____

_____

_____

_____

_____

_____

_____

_____

_____

_____

_____

_____

_____

Awaken the Awe

Therefore let us be grateful for receiving a kingdom that cannot be shaken, and thus let us offer to God acceptable worship, with reverence and awe, for our God is a consuming fire.

Hebrews 12:28–29

But the hour is coming, and is now here, when the true worshipers will worship the Father in spirit and truth, for the Father is seeking such people to worship him.

John 4:23

All these things my hand has made, and so all these things came to be, declares the Lord. But this is the one to whom I will look: he who is humble and contrite in spirit and trembles at my word.

Isaiah 66:2

Oh come, let us worship and bow down; let us kneel before the Lord, our Maker!

Psalm 95:6

THINK ABOUT THE TIMES IN YOUR LIFE THAT YOU FOUND yourself in total awe of something, so blown away by the magnitude of a gesture, a story or place that you had to collect yourself. A time when the only proper reaction was "Wow!"

Maybe it was a biography story on television where you saw immeasurable sacrifice in another person with incredible results. Perhaps you found yourself next to an ocean or on a mountaintop where the glory of nature was on full display. The day your child was born. The day you were the recipient of a gift that was life-changing, more than you could have ever hoped for.

The specific situations that create this sense of awe are different for all of us, our stories are unique, but, we've all been there.

By definition, "awe," is a feeling of reverential respect mixed with fear or wonder.

The experiences above all fit the bill. They invoke a sense of awe for a number of reasons, but one is that they make us feel small. They remind us of where our own abilities end and bring the fragility of life into full focus. In these moments, we're forced to focus on something so much bigger and more amazing than ourselves that any reaction other than full-hearted, reverential respect, fear and wonder just seems inadequate.

When is the last time you opened your heart to allow the Christmas story to bring your heart and emotions to the same place? I know I certainly fall short in this area. By getting so caught up in the traditions, shopping, baking and worldly preparations, I lose the ability to experience the story—the truth—the way I should. But, every now and then, a candlelight service or other situation, where everything else is drowned out, brings it back.

Maybe with a little refocusing and re-centering, we could all bring that feeling back into the rest of the season, rather than reserving it for forced situations alone.

According to today's scriptures, worshipers who worship with this sense of awe are the ones God seeks. He designed us with the ability to experience this wonder to better understand his holiness, his might, and his glory. When we take the Christmas story, the beginning of the story of our own salvation and reconciliation with God, for granted—leaving out amazement, fear and wonder—we're doing ourselves and our Savior a disservice.

So, where do we start?

First, like every other endeavor worth tackling, we ask our Father to open our hearts and our eyes, and to draw near to us as we draw near to him.

On a personal level, ask him to remind you of the magnitude of that night, when the Savior of this world and our hearts was born of a virgin to ultimately save you from the sin of this world that would be impossible for you to shed on your own.

Then, imagine yourself in that place. Think about the darkness of that night that mimics your own heart, and about the light found nestled in swaddling cloths in a manger, and the promise he carried and eventually fulfilled.

That is what we celebrate, what we should prepare our hearts for. Are you willing to open your heart to the awe of it all?

Journal

Read Luke chapters 1 and 2. Take your time. Highlight or write down aspects of the story that you often glaze over or may have missed before. Write down what they mean to you, and your relationship with God, today.

_____

_____

_____

_____

_____

_____

_____

_____

_____

_____

_____

_____

_____

Cling to Past Promises; Anticipate the Future

And again Isaiah says, "The root of Jesse will come, even he who arises to rule the Gentiles; in him will the Gentiles hope." May the God of hope fill you with all joy and peace in believing, so that by the power of the Holy Spirit you may abound in hope.

Romans 15:12–13

THINGS WILL GET BETTER."

"This is a storm; it will pass."

"There's something better just around the corner."

"This just wasn't the right opportunity."

When you've found yourself struggling, I mean *really* struggling, how often have you heard these well-meaning phrases as a response? How often have you been reminded that your current thoughts, feelings and emotions are merely temporary?

Maybe they are. This whole life is temporary, something Christians are reminded of frequently to allow us to anticipate the future, eternal hope we have to look forward to long after the things of this world pass away.

However, if our vision is fully forward-facing, we might be missing a foundational aspect of hope—one necessary to better anticipate the future: the past.

Bear with me.

In the verses for today, the Apostle Paul quotes the Old Testament book of Isaiah, prophesying the future arrival of the one in whom the Gentiles would hope. He then blesses the recipients of his message, asking the God of hope to fill them with joy and peace as they trust, allowing them to overflow with hope by the power of the Holy Spirit.

He is reminding them that their hope, foretold long before Christ's arrival, had come, bringing with him something far more powerful than they could imagine on their own.

He's reminding them to base their hope on the past, on the one who had already come.

How relevant is this to our current season of Advent? We are looking forward with anticipation to celebrating the arrival of the same Savior, born long ago, yet foretold by the prophets long before even that.

To understand, grasp and cling to our future hope, looking forward is essential. But, the hope we find can only be complete by basing it on the arrival of Jesus, by looking back.

Regardless of the situations you're facing today, your hope has come. Draw near to God today by thanking him for this complex, yet all encompassing hope that covers your past and your future.

Journal

What does "hope" mean to you? What are your greatest hopes? How is your perspective changed by centering and placing that hope in God? What is he revealing to you today?

Remember the Light

The Lord *is my light and my salvation; whom shall I fear? The* Lord *is the stronghold of my life; of whom shall I be afraid?*

Psalm 27:1

Again Jesus spoke to them, saying, "I am the light of the world. Whoever follows me will not walk in darkness but will have the light of life."

John 8:12

In the same way, let your light shine before others, so that they may see your good works and give glory to your Father who is in heaven.

Matthew 5:16

DON'T YOU LOVE CRYSTAL CLEAR NIGHTS, whether at home or out in a secluded spot in nature? Nights where the stars just shine clearer and brighter than other nights? These are nights where light pollution is reduced, the moon is hidden, and nothing stands between you and one of this world's most spectacular views. They're simply awe-inspiring.

Now, imagine that crystal clear ancient sky over Bethlehem when a star guided the Magi to Jesus, in the arms of his mother. It's inspiring to think about and is no wonder that we've sung Christmas songs, read poems and have appreciated art that features it for generations since.

That single star was sent by God to guide those in Bible times, and us today, to so much more. It was just the beginning, the beginning of it all.

Jesus came to be a light to the world, a teacher who would lead his followers, both then and now, to relationships with God, eventually laying down his life to atone for their—and our own—sins.

We see his role as a light to the world in the verses above and are reminded of the promise that whoever walks in the light cannot be overcome by darkness.

As followers, understanding Jesus's role as a light, starting with that single star over Bethlehem, is just the start. You see... our world? It needs that light more than—perhaps—ever before. For some, the only—or first—chance they'll have to experience it, is through us: followers of the ultimate Light, who hold on to it, believe in it and trust in it, despite the dark circumstances and situations we find ourselves in.

Jesus was and is the Light, but Matthew 5:16 tells us that we are to let our light shine before others, allowing them to glorify the Father in heaven through our actions. Because Jesus was sent as *the* Light to our world, destined to point us toward and reconcile us with God in heaven, we are able to shine the same light to others, spreading hope and the Gospel message of joy, truth and salvation.

So, do we do it? Or, do we find ways to live in, hide in, or get lost in the darkness of this world, allowing it to consume us, rather than remembering the Light of the world that cannot be consumed by darkness, reflecting it outward to others as we are commanded to do?

We, by God's grace and with his leading, can do better!

Today, while drawing near to God by dwelling on the idea of light, let's ask him to allow us to shine his light to those around us, while taking comfort in the fact that, in him, there is no darkness at all.

Journal

When you think of perfect light, what comes to mind? What emotions does that image bring up for you? As you think, make a list of friends, co-workers and/or loved ones who could use God's light in their lives. Ask him to use you to reflect his light through everyday encounters and conversations.

Sing of His Love

I will sing of the steadfast love of the LORD, forever; with my mouth I will make known your faithfulness to all generations. For I said, "Steadfast love will be built up forever; in the heavens you will establish your faithfulness." You have said, "I have made a covenant with my chosen one; I have sworn to David my servant: 'I will establish your offspring forever, and build your throne for all generations.'"

Let the heavens praise your wonders, O LORD, your faithfulness in the assembly of the holy ones! For who in the skies can be compared to the LORD? Who among the heavenly beings is like the LORD, a God greatly to be feared in the council of the holy ones, and awesome above all who are around him? O LORD God of hosts, who is mighty as you are, O LORD, with your faithfulness all around you?

Psalm 89:1–8

DO YOU EVER FEEL SMALL IN THE GRAND SCHEME OF things?

There's a lot going on in our world—on both a personal and global level. We read stories that induce fear. We feel out of control. We wish, hope and pray that we can be a part of the solution, yet we often wonder how we can even begin to make a difference.

Unfortunately, we sometimes transfer these feelings, our own feelings of inadequacy and "smallness," onto our God.

We look at our surroundings and listen to the definitions and descriptions the world uses to describe anything relating to the spiritual realm and we forget one of the most important, eternal truths: He. Loves. Us.

In today's Psalm, Ethan the Ezrahite takes time to praise God for his love. To rejoice in the fact that his love stands firm throughout his shifting world. To recognize the fact that among the holiest of the holy realm, God is greatly feared and more awesome than all.

He also points out something that should matter to us this Advent season. He references God's covenant with David, which points forward to the New Testament coming of the Christ child, the first coming we celebrate as we move closer to Christmas day this year and every year.

Our God? Our God is all-holy. All knowing. All powerful. All good.

There is not a thread of weakness in his being. Not an ounce of misguided motivation. Not a single quality that we should question or doubt.

And—perhaps—the most amazing part of God's incomparable being is this: he loves us. He wants and call us to be a part of his story, a story written long before any of us came to be.

It's time for us to stop painting our own picture of who God is, to stop assigning human qualities to the one without them. It's time for us to simply reflect on his love and to draw near to a goodness that is often—maybe always—hard for us to even comprehend.

Today, reflect on God's love, the love that allowed the all-powerful God of the universe to send his own son into our world to save us and draw us closer to him. It's time to sing of the love that is truer than all others, until there's no other song we could possibly sing.

Journal

What does this kind of love mean to you? How—on a personal level—
has God demonstrated his love for you?

_____

_____

_____

_____

_____

_____

_____

_____

_____

_____

_____

_____

_____

_____

Take Shelter, Find Peace

For to us a child is born, to us a son is given; and the government shall be upon his shoulder, and his name shall be called Wonderful Counselor, Mighty God, Everlasting Father, Prince of Peace.

Isaiah 9:6

You keep him in perfect peace whose mind is stayed on you, because he trusts in you.

Isaiah 26:3

O LORD, you will ordain peace for us, for you have indeed done for us all our works.

Isaiah 26:12

For he himself is our peace, who has made us both one and has broken down in his flesh the dividing wall of hostility.

Ephesians 2:14

PEACE IS SUCH A BEAUTIFUL HOLIDAY THEME, isn't it? It brings to mind nights reading near a fireplace. Snow falling silently outside. Hot chocolate and cookie baking with family, full of laughter and newly-minted memories.

The key to many of these—admittedly over-idealized—images of peace is shelter, right? Shelter from whatever storm or weather is raging outside. Warmth that comes from being separated from the elements, whether they are caused by nature or more worldly conflicts.

Peace is often rooted in shelter, and the sense of safety and serenity it creates.

Sometimes, much like the quiet we reflected on a few days ago, peace from the storms that surround us can seem more desirable yet less obtainable than others. Yet, we still long for it.

I know I do. About 8 years ago, my husband and I made the decision that I would branch out on my own, leaving the comfortable non-profit organization that I was working for, to start my own business. The pretty picture we painted in our minds included flexible hours, spending extra time with our kids, keeping the house clean and more... the best of both the "working" and the "staying home" worlds.

Fast forward.

Today, my "flexible" hours are more than full time and our family has expanded in size exponentially. I'm on call for clients at hours I never imagined, doing work I love, with the ability God gave me. But... sometimes, it spirals. My kids need and deserve a mom whose attention is theirs. The laundry piles higher than I'd like to admit, and sometimes deadlines loom a little too close for comfort. There are times—even doing what I know God led me to—that my heart yearns for peace.

No matter what your situation is, your "crazy," I'm sure you feel the same!

But... I don't think I always go about looking for that peace in the right place.

Let's look back at today's scripture.

This series of passages is like a funnel, with our Savior at the start and our source of peace (spoiler alert: still him) at the end.

Look closer. Jesus was sent into this world to be many things. One of these, prophesied in the book of Isaiah, is the Prince of Peace. This is made possible by God's role of keeping in perfect peace those who trust in him. The passages strip away our role in our accomplishments—including our successes and searches for peace—by making it clear that anything *we* have done, is really only by *his* doing. Finally, they close out by pointing us to the only true source of peace: the Son himself.

Read through them again.

How off track are we when we search for peace in this world, without bringing Jesus Christ's arrival, sent to serve, to teach, to connect the law and grace and to bring us back to our creator? How could peace possibly spring from any other source?

Things in this world, like those scenes we pictured earlier, can be peaceful, but they cannot bring true, lasting peace that depends not on us at all, but, in our steadfast trust in our Savior.

Today, ask God to reveal his peace—through his Son—to you and to remind you of his presence in your life. Draw near to him by reflecting on his role as the only real source of peace.

Journal

Write down the stressors in your life, and your concerns—the things that occupy your mind, even amidst the most peaceful scenario you can envision. Thank God for his role as your hope and peace while laying those things at his feet.

Be Refined to Reflect

"Behold, I send my messenger, and he will prepare the way before me. And the Lord *whom you seek will suddenly come to his temple; and the messenger of the covenant in whom you delight, behold, he is coming, says the* Lord *of hosts. But who can endure the day of his coming, and who can stand when he appears? For he is like a refiner's fire and like fullers' soap. He will sit as a refiner and purifier of silver, and he will purify the sons of Levi and refine them like gold and silver, and they will bring offerings in righteousness to the* Lord. *Then the offering of Judah and Jerusalem will be pleasing to the* Lord *as in the days of old as in former years.*

"Then I will draw near to you for judgment. I will be a swift witness against the sorcerers, against the adulterers, against those who swear falsely, against those who oppress the hired worker in his wages, the widow and the fatherless, against those who thrust alongside the sojourner, and do not fear me, says the Lord *of hosts.*

"For I the Lord *do not change; therefore you, O children of Jacob, are not consumed."*

Malachi 3:1–6

I N THE CHRISTIAN WALK, we don't often think of the process of purification as a positive thing. We are taught to expect trials and hardships, and we understand (though we don't always accept) that in all things, God is working for our good and his plan.

I grew up with a head-deep knowledge of these things. But, it didn't click until I went to a youth conference in high school. What I learned there took a while to sink in, but, has since come to my mind and heart in many situations.

It starts with the verses above, where God's role as a "refiner and purifier of silver" is referenced. To understand this, we first need to understand what process silver goes through to be refined—made pure.

During refining, silver is heated to a temperature that allows particles and impurities to come to the surface, where they are removed by the refiner. It's then allowed to rest until the next round, where the process is repeated, time and time again. Silver is only considered pure when the refiner can see his or her face in its reflection.

Ironically, or perhaps not ironically at all, the process is often referred to as "testing." That's right, silver is not pure until it has been repeatedly tested, seemingly to its very limits.

How appropriate then, is it, for Biblical writers and prophets to refer to God's refining role in our lives? We are essentially told that we will be tested and tried until we reflect our maker, our Savior, our God.

How often do we consider this during the process, when we are tested by circumstances so much bigger than ourselves, to our own perceived limits? How often do we thank God for his refining presence in our lives, remembering the promises he has in store for those of us who accept his leading and finish well?

I know that I definitely fall short in this area. I tend to resort to anger, frustration and hopelessness, instead of considering how the really tough parts of this life help me know my Lord, reflect his glory and spread his message of truth. What about you?

What if we, as followers of God, focused on sharing his truths and eternal promises, instead of falling into worldly responses to trials? Imagine the impact a movement like this could create for the Kingdom of God! Isn't it exciting to consider?

Draw near this Advent by drawing near to *all* of who God is and *every* role he plays in our lives. Consider the fact that only a God who truly desires our hearts and wants the very best for us would be patient enough—despite *our* impatience—to carry out a process like this.

Our God is a refiner; I challenge you to praise him for it, today.

Journal

How has God been working to refine your heart this year? Are you allowing the process to better reflect his presence in your life? Ask God to open your heart and your eyes to use the hardships you're facing to make you more like him.

Rejoice in Fear

There shall come forth a shoot from the stump of Jesse, and a branch from his roots shall bear fruit. And the Spirit of the LORD shall rest upon him, the Spirit of wisdom and understanding, the Spirit of counsel and might, the Spirit of knowledge and the fear of the LORD. And his delight shall be in the fear of the LORD. He shall not judge by what his eyes see, or decide disputes by what his ears hear, but with righteousness he shall judge the poor, and decide with equity for the meek of the earth; and he shall strike the earth with the rod of his mouth, and with the breath of his lips he shall kill the wicked. Righteousness shall be the belt of his waist, and faithfulness the belt of his loins. The wolf shall dwell with the lamb, and the leopard shall lie down with the young goat, and the calf and the lion and the fattened calf together; and a little child shall lead them. The cow and the bear shall graze; their young shall lie down together; and the lion shall eat straw like the ox. The nursing child shall play over the hole of the cobra, and the weaned child shall put his hand on the adder's den. They shall not hurt or destroy in all my holy mountain; for the earth shall be full of the knowledge of the LORD as the waters cover the sea. In that day the root of Jesse, who shall stand as a signal for the peoples—of him shall the nations inquire, and his resting place shall be glorious.

Isaiah 11:1–10

WHAT THINGS DO YOU FEAR? Not phobias, necessarily, or things that make you anxious. I'm talking straight, raw fear.

What stops you in your tracks, causing rational thoughts to cease and next steps hard to put together?

That thing—whatever it is—and the feeling it causes probably isn't your first thought when you think about God. No, the God we've been taught to consider as a big, loving, embracing, father figure in the sky, probably doesn't incite raw fear.

Maybe that's because—somewhere along the line—we've gone off track.

Let's consider Biblical encounters with God. One that immediately comes to mind for me, is John's vision of God in the book of Revelation (1:17): *When I saw him, I fell at his feet as though dead.* Or, Isaiah's vision of the Lord in chapter 6: *"Woe to me!" I cried. "I am ruined!"* Moses's response to God's presence is also one of fear. In Exodus chapter 3 (verse 6) he covers his face because he was *afraid to look at God.*

These responses are not the traditional fear-based responses we're used to, not the fear of horror movies, yet, they're still rooted in raw, real fear.

Fearing the Lord is mentioned several times in scripture, but, I am not sure we connect that command with the fear these individuals experienced during their own encounters.

The cultural norm we've accepted, of God as an all-loving father who desires our hearts, is true. But, it's just a part of the story. In wholly accepting it, we forget about God's power, that his mere thoughts and words brought about every single thing in the known and unknown universe. We forget that he is sometimes described in terms of his wrath and the vengeance he will seek. Most importantly, we forget that our single-dimensional, selfish, mortal selves are *so far* from his perfection, his radiance, his holiness, that we can't even grasp it.

In order to draw near to him with the respect and honor he deserves, we must be willing to accept all of God's qualities. We must understand that the conflict we feel in the difference between his *love* and the *fear* we are called to delight in, is a conflict we create on our own, through our own limitations. Without his awe- and fear-inducing power and holiness, his love for us would not be as all-encompassing and complete as it is.

Only when we learn to fear God can we truly delight in the fact that he loved us—and still loves us—enough to send his only Son to be born in a manger, grow in human form, teach us, and become the only acceptable, perfect sacrifice for our shortcomings and sins.

Does the thought of God's perfect power and holiness cause you to fall to the ground in fear? To tremble? To weep? If not, it might be time for a shift in perspective. Today is a great day to start by considering how you might improve in rejoicing and delighting in the fear of the Lord.

Journal

List the qualities of God that you can come up with in the next thirty seconds or so. If you need a jump start, run a quick online search. Pick five to reflect on for a bit, then, come back. Write about what feelings these qualities create for you, then, thank God for them. Write how these qualities could help change the way you see him and the way he works in your life.

Become a Servant

And he said to them, "The kings of the Gentiles exercise lordship over them, and those in authority over them are called benefactors. But not so with you. Rather, let the greatest among you become as the youngest, and the leader as one who serves."

Luke 22:25–26

It shall not be so among you. But whoever would be great among you must be your servant, and whoever would be first among you must be your slave, even as the Son of Man came not to be served but to serve and to give his life as a ransom for many.

Matthew 20:26–28

When he had washed their feet and put on his outer garments and resumed his place, he said to them, "Do you understand what I have done to you? You call me Teacher and Lord, and you are right, for so I am. If I then, your Lord and Teacher, have washed your feet, you also ought to wash one another's feet. For I have given you an example, that you also should do just as I have done to you. Truly, truly, I say to you, a servant is not greater than his master, nor is a messenger greater than the one who sent him. If you know these things, blessed are you if you do them.

John 13:12–17

W E'VE ALL BEEN EXPOSED TO VARIOUS LEADERSHIP styles, in the workplace, in the church, even in personal or familial roles. Some resonate with us, challenging us and encouraging us to action; they motivate our desire to follow by inspiring us in one way or another. Others? Not so much. Instead of inspiring us to reach for new heights, they earn eye rolls and side comments while feeding inner resentment.

Leaders can be despised for a number of reasons. But, those who reach the status of "inspirational," often have something in common, a quality that stands out: they care. They know their purpose and can challenge their teams to push toward a specific goal, but, they also have hearts and are willing to let them show when appropriate.

One way some leaders show heart? Through service.

This service might look different in different settings or groups:

A leader of a Bible study or book club organizing a meal train for someone in need.

A father willing to drop everything to help his adult child with a handy-man task.

A neighbor taking time out of his or her day to drive another neighbor in need to an appointment.

A pastor serving at a local soup kitchen.

A CEO taking time out to listen to the personal needs of an employee, then aiding in creating a solution.

Or, something else entirely.

I've seen each of the situations above play out and have always felt inspired when a leader's servant heart shines through.

But, for the greatest example of a leader with a servant's heart—a *perfect* example of a servant leader—we should set our sights higher, toward the servant leadership seen in the Christ child (and adult) himself, Jesus.

Today's passages are isolated descriptions and just a few of the many examples of Jesus's servant heart in action. His acts of servanthood, from washing the feet of his disciples to listening and spending time with the lowest of the low, to his persistent sharing and spreading of the truths of the Spirit to his ultimate sacrifice on the cross are amazing and awe-inspiring.

They are also more than stories or simple collections of words that point us toward our Father in heaven: they're guidelines by which we should aspire to live.

Jesus came to spread truth and to bridge the gap between sinful man and wholly perfect God. His life serves as a blueprint meant to mold us... the only worthwhile example for us to follow. Understanding his life, his stories and his mission is only part one. Unless we change our aspirations—leading by example through servanthood being one of them—our mission to reflect his light and love to the world will fall short.

Becoming a servant is hard, mostly because it's so unnatural for us. We thrive—we think—when we impress others, when we live picture-perfect lives, or, when our achievements leave others aspiring to be like us, rather than our Father.

We have it backwards when we allow our society and surroundings to lead us further and further in the wrong direction.

Wouldn't this season, traditionally filled with desiring all the *wrong* things, be a great time to make it right? To make small steps toward placing the needs of others above our own wants and desires? What a beautiful picture of drawing near to the only true source of love and light in this world!

Are you willing to become a servant to better reflect God's love this season and beyond?

Journal

Make a list of ten intentional actions you could complete over the next month or so to serve others. Commit to at least 4. Ask God to give you a willing, cheerful heart as you serve, allowing you to be a reflection of his love as you set off.

Come Delight

"Come, everyone who thirsts, come to the waters; and he who has no money, come, buy and eat! Come, buy wine and milk without money and without price. Why do you spend your money for that which is not bread, and your labor for that which does not satisfy? Listen diligently to me, and eat what is good, and delight yourselves in rich food. Incline your ear, and come to me; hear, that your soul may live; and I will make with you an everlasting covenant, my steadfast, sure love for David."

Isaiah 55:1–3

HOW MANY NIGHTS DO YOU GO TO BED COMPLETELY SPENT? Totally drained?

You reflect on your mishaps of the day: the harsh tone you used with your children, spouse or significant other. Your unwilling heart at work. That bit of gossip you should have put an end to. You count your errors and head off to sleep feeling "less than" and empty. You vow to do better tomorrow.

But then, tomorrow arrives. You fall into the same pattern and the emptiness continues to set in.

Maybe you head to God's word. But, maybe you head the other way... toward the world. You might not even know you're doing it.

The world subtly—and not so subtly—points out our inadequacies on a constant basis. Without the flawless body, 9–5 job, 2.3 perfect children and white picket fence, you must be falling short. But, ask anyone who has achieved those things and—if they're honest—they'll tell you they feel the same emptiness at the end of the day that you do.

This season seems to make it even worse. Ever find yourself debating whether or not you need a new, bigger television just because there's a great deal? Or, suddenly dropping hints about chocolate diamonds because a commercial made you feel warm and fuzzy? I have.

Where do desires like these come from? I'm willing to bet they start with a search for joy, for fullness that this world—even the best of it—can't satisfy and never will.

In today's scripture verses, God speaks through his prophet, demanding those with nothing, those hungry, weak and empty, to come to him... to draw near.

He doesn't promise to give them the minimum they require. No. He promises splendor, life in abundance. Most importantly, he points them forward, to the coming savior we celebrate this season, toward his everlasting covenant with David.

In those verses, God is speaking to his people, the Israelites. But, he's also speaking to you and me, today.

We may have food. We may not thirst. But, we understand hopelessness. We understand hurt. We understand pushing ourselves so hard to succeed that we end up broken, not sure of how to even start putting the pieces back together.

The worst part? We live with constant "solutions" that are ready for us to choose from. Our friends have all been there and offer well-meaning but often misguided solutions. Television shows demonstrate that a few nights out, vent sessions and bottom-of-the-barrel moments will let us "get it out" so that we can "get back on track." Social media gurus and fitness icons tell us if we just try harder, we'll find the happiness we crave.

Fortunately—since none of these solutions ever truly pays off—scripture offers something *so much* more. This time of year is the perfect time to dwell on it, soak it in and claim its truth.

Our good, good Father invites us, no matter our hurt, no matter our struggle, no matter our sin or weakness, to come to him, to seek him first. It might not mean smooth sailing or a life without hurt, certainly not immunity to the world. Far from it in many cases. It *does* mean a fullness that cannot be found elsewhere. It means an abundance in spirit. A complete joy. A hope that surpasses all temporary, worldly hopes.

Our role in it all? "Come." Draw near. Allow the filling to begin. When you feel that sense of emptiness creeping back in, offer it up to God again and again and he will fill you with what you really need.

The Christ has come. The covenant has been fulfilled. Leave emptiness behind and find abundance in these truths, today.

Journal

Write down the ways you're feeling empty today. In what ways has the holiday rush added to these feelings? What biblical truths could you use to combat these feelings and replace them with God's truth?

_____

_____

_____

_____

_____

_____

_____

_____

_____

_____

_____

_____

_____

Plant a Garden of Hope

And again Isaiah says, "The root of Jesse will come, even he who arises to rule the Gentiles; in him will the Gentiles hope." May the God of hope fill you with all joy and peace in believing so that by the power of the Holy Spirit you may abound in hope.

Romans 15:12–13

WHAT DOES FALL MEAN TO YOU? I know we're rapidly approaching the official start of winter, but stick with me.

I'll let you in on a secret that you might be able to relate to: I love the Advent season. But... it might be the only thing about the soon-to-be-upon-us winter that I enjoy. The prospect of months inside, can't-feel-your-face cold and short, dark days is not something I'm great at looking forward to.

But, there's something about fall that I do enjoy: the hope of spring. I know it sounds silly, however, there's a tangible way I put it to action.

I plant bulbs.

I enjoy researching bulbs that will grow well in my area and getting them in the ground. I picture what they'll look like as they grow and bloom. I anticipate their colors... their fragrances... the bigger picture.

As the cold sets in, I enjoy walking around what I've planted and often find myself smiling as I wonder which ones will grow and how they'll look as they start to peek through the soil—or melting snow—when warmer weather arrives.

Can you relate? Do you find yourself looking forward with hope during various—literal or figurative—seasons of life?

The Advent season is a time of hope as well, a hope much greater than flowers.

In the verses above, Paul references Isaiah's earlier prophecy that the root of Jesse would spring up, the one who would bring hope to the Gentiles.

He used this passage to demonstrate the fulfillment of the prophecy through Jesus Christ's birth, death and resurrection. He then urges believers to allow that God-sent hope to fill them with peace and joy to the point of overflowing (verse 13, in the NIV translation of scripture is phrased "*May the God of hope fill you with all joy and peace as you trust in him, so that you may overflow with hope by the power of the Holy Spirit*").

This, friends, is one outlandishly amazing and beautiful concept.

So often, we cling to the hope of the future. To the hope of our own ambitions. To the hope in promises made by other, fallible, humans. To the hope of an unknown future. What are these hopes rooted in? Arguably, nothing.

As believers, we can—and should—hope in something so much greater. Our hope has come. His roots are eternal. His miraculous birth, death and resurrection provide proof that, while our earthly futures are uncertain and temporary, our forever is already written, purchased by a Savior born in a manger two-thousand years ago.

Today, examine your heart. Is God the source of your hope? Can you overflow with peace and joy, knowing your hope has already come?

Journal

Sketch out a picture, or describe in words, what hope means to you. In what area of your life could you use peace this Advent season? In what ways has God already worked in your life, that you could cling to during current and future obstacles?

_____

_____

_____

_____

_____

_____

_____

_____

_____

_____

_____

_____

_____

Wait with Confidence

The LORD is good to those who wait for him, to the soul who seeks him.

Lamentations 3:25

Therefore the LORD waits to be gracious to you, and therefore he exalts himself to show mercy to you. For the LORD is a God of justice; blessed are all those who wait for him.

Isaiah 30:18

But they who wait for the LORD shall renew their strength; they shall mount up with wings like eagles; they shall run and not be weary; they shall walk and not faint.

Isaiah 40:31

THE WAITING PLACE.

Whether you've spent much time recently with your nose in Dr. Seuss books or not, you might recall "The Waiting Place," from preschool-to-college-graduation gift favorite, "The Places You'll Go."

While his spin on that place is whimsical and fun, waiting places in our own lives are usually less so. Yet, they're familiar... aren't we all waiting for something? For loved ones to return home? For positive outcomes on tests? For healing?

Relief? New opportunities? Vacations? Adventure? No matter who you are, you're probably waiting for something right now!

Good news: we're in great company. Abraham was 100 years old when his firstborn arrived. Jacob waited 14 years for Rachel's hand. The Israelites endured a few hundred years of slavery then 40 years wandering in the desert before reaching the promised land.

The process can be hard. Unknowns are rarely classified as "fun," yet, they serve a purpose. The Bible is filled with promises of rewards for waiting well, as well as the eye-opening truth that waiting for God's desired outcome (much like the refining process we discussed a few days ago), will always result in more than we could imagine on our own.

How appropriate is it, then, to focus on waiting well during the Advent, or the arrival of the ultimate blessing: Jesus Christ?

Upon his arrival, the Jews had been waiting for their king, their Messiah, for centuries. During periods of slavery, captivity, wandering and even exile, these people, from generation to generation, awaited their promised Savior. Many of the verses above refer to this event, as it was foretold by the prophets throughout history.

Though, many of them failed to wait well. They followed false religions and false gods because the hope of a Messiah was far too far away, far too hard, for them. They broke commandments. They didn't heed the warnings of the prophets. Many failed.

What a blessing it is for us during our own periods of waiting, especially during this season, to be able to see the bigger picture. We can look back on the fulfillment of the prophecies and God's promises while looking forward to the promises yet to be fulfilled, with confidence!

We may not be able to see what our own periods of waiting will result in, but, we can know that, by trusting in God's plan and waiting well, while following his leading in our lives, that his plan *will* come to fruition and we will be blessed—

whether here or in heaven—for waiting well while aligning our desires with our Father's desires.

We can choose to wait well, drawing near to God as we cast our cares on him, believing in his perfect will, both during this season and in the future.

Journal

Review today's scriptures again. After doing so, make a list of things, answers, situations or resolutions you're waiting on. Next to that list, write out the promises in those scriptures—and others if you're feeling ambitious—for waiting well. Ask God to work in your heart as you wait on his will and his timing.

Learn to Follow:
A Willing Submission

To you, O LORD, I lift up my soul. O my God, in you I trust; let me not be put to shame; let not my enemies exult over me. Indeed, none who wait for you shall be put to shame; they shall be ashamed who are wantonly treacherous.

Make me to know your ways, O LORD; teach me your paths. Lead me in your truth and teach me, for you are the God of my salvation; for you I wait all the day long. Remember your mercy, O LORD, and your steadfast love, for they have been from of old. Remember not the sins of my youth or my transgressions; according to your steadfast love remember me, for the sake of your goodness, O LORD!

Good and upright is the LORD; therefore he instructs sinners in the way. He leads the humble in what is right, and teaches the humble his way. All the paths of the LORD are steadfast love and faithfulness, for those who keep his covenant and his testimonies.

For your name's sake, O LORD, pardon my guilt, for it is great. Who is the man who fears the LORD? Him will he instruct in the way that he should choose. His soul shall abide in well-being, and his offspring shall inherit the land. The friendship of the LORD is for those who fear him, and he makes known to them his covenant. My eyes are ever toward the LORD, for he will pluck my feet out of the net.

Turn to me and be gracious to me, for I am lonely and afflicted. The troubles of my heart are enlarged; bring me out of my distresses. Consider my affliction and my trouble, and forgive all my sins.

Consider how many are my foes, and with what violent hatred they hate me. Oh, guard my soul, and deliver me! Let me not be put to shame, for I take refuge in you. May integrity and uprightness preserve me, for I wait for you.

Redeem Israel, O God, out of all his troubles.

Psalm 25:1–22

W E AREN'T TRAINED TO FOLLOW.
Today, "following" has, in many cases, become synonymous with weakness.

Women promising to submit to their husbands in wedding vows? Outdated.

Children who are content to let others take the reins? Concerning.

Men content in their current career roles, not pushing for the next big move? Uninspiring.

As a result, we've become a people taught to challenge authority and societal norms. We've been programmed to question those with higher statuses than our own. We've even learned to hide any part of ourselves that screams "follower" for fear of the feedback we might receive.

In some ways, this drive to lead can be a positive. It helps us push for innovation and change. It gives us confidence when sharing what is right, even if it's unpopular. It drives us forward.

However, when we lose our ability to follow when necessary, to submit, we could be hindering our relationship with God.

In some areas, especially in our walks with God, being a follower might just be a critical strength.

Think of David. David was a king, a warrior, a leader among his people. Without the ability to lead, he would have accomplished very little. But, he understood whole-hearted submission to God.

One of my favorite scripture passages is found in 2 Samuel, chapter six. Here David, with undignified abandon, disregarding the reactions of those around him—including his own wife—dances before the Lord with wholehearted abandon. His only thought? Full submission and praise to his God.

We see this sort of willing submission again in today's verses from Psalm 25. You see, David understood that his authority pertained to earthly matters alone, and that without God's provision and guidance, he would be lost.

Following may not have come easy to David, but, he understood its importance. He asked God to guide him, to teach him, to instruct him. He understood that only in following God could his anguish, distress and afflictions be relieved. His hope was in the Lord, made possible by submission and a willingness to follow.

It's easy to understand God's authority and his role as our creator... but, are we truly willing to admit our own smallness and neediness, in light of his greatness and love? Are we willing to become followers, submitting to his will, even when we can't understand it, or if our own desires scream at us to go a different way?

Only through submission can our will become entwined and aligned with the will of our Father. His refuge and goodness are readily available, yet, our willingness to follow is essential to see them prevail.

Today, draw near to God by giving him your struggles and need to lead. Ask him to be your strength, submitting fully to his will.

Journal

What are the words you associate with "submission?" What does sub-mitting to God look like to you? What parts of this process are the most challenging for you? Ask God to remove these roadblocks so that you may willingly follow him, today.

Stop Planning:
Be Led

And a vision appeared to Paul in the night: a man of Macedonia was standing there, urging him and saying, "Come over to Macedonia and help us." And when Paul had seen the vision, immediately we sought to go on into Macedonia, concluding that God had called us to preach the gospel to them.

Acts 16:9–10

Therefore, Eli said to Samuel, "Go, lie down, and if he calls you, you shall say, 'Speak LORD, for your servant hears.'" So Samuel went and lay down in his place. And the LORD came and stood, calling as at other times, "Samuel! Samuel!" And Samuel said, "Speak for your servant hears." ... And the word of Samuel came to all Israel.

1 Samuel 3:9–10, 4:1a

And her husband, Joseph, being a just man and unwilling to put her to shame, resolved to divorce her quietly. But as he considered these things, behold, an angel of the Lord appeared to him in a dream, saying, "Joseph, son of David, do not fear to take Mary as your wife, for that which is conceived in her is from the Holy Spirit. She will bear a son, and you shall call his name Jesus, for he will save his people from their sins. All this took place to fulfill what the Lord had spoken by the prophet: "Behold, the virgin shall conceive and bear a son, and they shall call his name Immanuel" (which means, God with us). When Joseph woke from sleep, he did as the angel of the Lord commanded him: he took his wife, but knew her not until she had given birth to a son. And he called his name Jesus.

Matthew 1:19–25

"IF YOU WANT TO HEAR GOD LAUGH, TELL HIM YOUR PLANS."

You've heard it before, right? We all have. While the motives might sometimes be misaligned, the idea is spot on.

We're raised, from a young age, to plan ahead. Some of us might hold on to that idea in a more compulsive manner than others, but, over time, we learn that planning ahead brings the "best" results.

How much time and energy have you put into planning for Christmas this year alone? For Christmas cards and gifts, for travel to see family and friends, for special events and dinners?

The holidays are just one example of how we plan—or attempt to plan—our lives. If I asked you where you hope to be in five years, I bet you'd have an answer.

Planning can be a positive thing. A life without schedules, plans and proactive thoughts would be chaotic at the very least. But, sometimes, these plans become our everything. They provide us more comfort than they should, something for us to cling to.

They can become so prominently featured in our lives that we forget something absolutely essential... we forget to listen; we lose our willingness to allow God to change our plans and direct our paths.

I included several scripture passages today (and could have included several more) because the scriptures are filled with examples of those who follow God's leading in their lives.

Each of these examples gives us a model that we ought to pay attention to.

These Biblical characters were individuals like us. They had hopes. They had dreams. They had *plans.*

But—where we often fall short—they listened intently to God's leading. They then followed what was spoken or revealed to them with big results: they each became vessels for God to fulfill *his* plans.

Listening to God's plan can be hard. We are surrounded by media, distractions and noise. Then, when we do feel his gentle nudging—or dramatic pushing—we often run back to the safety and certainty of our own plans. We fail to allow ourselves to submit to plans that differ from our own.

Sometimes—many times—this seems to work for us. It's easy to brush off a feeling as something we misunderstood... but in doing so, we might be missing out on something greater than we could ever imagine. Could you imagine what would have happened if Joseph went ahead with his original plan? Would God have still fulfilled his ultimate purpose? Certainly, but, imagine the blessings Joseph would have missed out on!

As our march through Advent continues, let's consider how much value we place on our own plans, and ask God to make us listeners who are willing to be led.

Journal

Have you felt God leading you toward something that doesn't match your own plans, or challenging you to change something in your life that you've been reluctant to act upon? What is it? Or have you ever listened to God's clear calling in your life? What were the results?

Day Twenty

Worship Him

Now after Jesus was born in Bethlehem of Judea in the days of Herod the king, behold, wise men from the east came to Jerusalem, saying, "Where is he who has been born king of the Jews? For we saw his star when it rose and have come to worship him." When Herod the king heard this, he was troubled, and all Jerusalem with him; and assembling all the chief priests and scribes of the people, he inquired of them where the Christ was to be born. They told him, "In Bethlehem of Judea, for so it is written by the prophet:

> *'And you, O Bethlehem, in the land of Judah, are by no means least among the rulers of Judah; for from you shall come a ruler who will shepherd my people Israel.'"*

Then Herod summoned the wise men secretly and ascertained from them what time the star had appeared. And he sent them to Bethlehem, saying, "Go and search diligently for the child, and when you have found him, bring me word, that I too may come and worship him." After listening to the king, they went on their way. And behold, the star that they had seen when it rose went before them until it came to rest over the place where the child was. When they saw the star, they rejoiced exceedingly with great joy. And going into the house, they saw the child with Mary his mother, and they fell down and worshiped him. Then,

opening their treasures, they offered him gifts, gold and frank-
incense and myrrh. And being warned in a dream not to return
to Herod, they departed to their own country by another way.

Matthew 2:1–12

ADMITTEDLY, today we're jumping a little ahead of our-selves, past the birth of our Savior and to the events that followed his birth. But this season is a season of preparation, which must include worship, so, it feels appro-priate.

Worship is integral to the Christian life. We search for churches, sometimes (perhaps incorrectly) judging their fit by the style of worship they present. We listen to worship music in our cars and homes by turning on the radio or playlist. We reflect on lyrics and Psalms when our hearts are burdened, overwhelmed or even joyful. It's a part of who we are.

Sometimes, though, it becomes such a part of us that we lose the sense of awe, the wonder and the focus that worship, in its truest sense, entails.

Consider the wise men of the Christmas story, described in today's passage from Matthew.

These men, so in tune with the words of the prophets and the signs in the world around them, were willing to drop eve-rything, journeying far from home toward an undisclosed ex-act location to find the King of the Jews (it's important to note that some scholars believe the wise men may have been Gen-tiles, making this mission—perhaps—even more significant).

When they arrived... they *worshipped.*

This passage describes them rejoicing exceedingly, with great joy, upon finding the child. As they encountered him, they bowed down and worshipped, presenting him with *treas-ures.*

Even more, they were so impacted—one might argue "changed" by their encounter—that, having been warned in a dream not to return to Herod, they took an alternate route home.

Is our worship awe-inspiring? Do we recognize that in worshipping our Lord, we are coming into the presence of our Savior, our King? Do we lay ourselves, and our treasures—our hopes, dreams and wants—on the ground in front of him in a show of true surrender, allowing the experience to change us and bring us close to him in a way that few other endeavors can?

Or, do we sing along with the words we know by heart, noting the tempo or pitch of the worship leader, then leave to go through our daily routine as normal?

Let's make a change. Let's make worship, *worship* again, remembering the significance of our God's eternal love for us and willingness to send his son to this world in human form, sent as a sacrifice that none other could ever be deemed worthy of. Let's allow God to work in our hearts and change us, drawing us closer to him.

Journal

Write out the lyrics of your favorite worship song, one you know by heart. Look at it, line by line, reflecting and highlighting words and phrases that stand out to you in new ways. Use those words and phrases to craft your own prayer of worship to God.

Day Twenty-One

Practicing Humility in a World that Celebrates Achievers

And Mary said, "My soul magnifies the Lord, and my spirit re-joices in God my Savior, for he has looked on the humble estate of his servant. For behold, from now on, all generations will call me blessed; for he who is mighty has done great things for me, and holy is his name. And his mercy is for those who fear him from generation to generation. He has shown strength with his arm; he has scattered the proud in the thoughts of their hearts; he has brought down the mighty from their thrones and exalted those of humble estate; he has filled the hungry with good things, and the rich he has sent away empty. He has helped his servant Israel, in remembrance of his mercy, as he spoke to our fathers, to Abraham and to his offspring forever."

Luke 1:46–55

WE ARE SURROUNDED BY PRESSURE. Pressure to get ahead or make that promotion at work. Pressure to put together Pinterest-worthy meals and de-signs at home. Pressure to own the best cars, the best houses. Pressure to "live our best lives." After all, Y.O.L.O.—right?

There are lots of old sayings and adages about the role of pressure in our lives. One, by Thomas Carlyle, reminds us: "No pressure. No diamonds."

Sometimes though—I would argue, many times—the pressure we feel, real, or, more than we'd like to admit it, perceived, breeds something else. It breeds pride and the need to be *just a little bit* better than others.

It fuels the entire social media movement. Do we post photos of screaming kids, of mediocre meals, of losing teams or lay-off notices? No, we use filters and sort through hundreds of takes to achieve the perfect angle. This even applies to Christmas morning, where we want our photos to reflect the most beautiful ornaments and the most HGTV-worthy, perfectly wrapped gifts.

Why?

Because we want to connect and engage those around us? No. Deep down, we want the "likes," the "loves," the "wows!" and other compliments that we've—by now—been programmed to chase. When we fail to hit the number or reactions we hoped for, we wonder why, and, as much as we might hate to admit it, our bent-to-achieve selves feel an innate sense of failure.

The Scriptures talk about pride and humility many, many times, telling us—like Paul—to boast only in Christ. Yet, I feel like the passage above, from the gospel of Luke, might be most relevant to our Advent journey.

Mary begins to understand the role God has chosen for her, selecting her to bring forth the child who would impact the world. We know this because she acknowledges it in verse 48: *for he has looked on the humble estate of his servant. For behold, from now on, all generations will call me blessed.*

That pride? It's rooted in the Lord and tied directly to his mightiness, his mercy and his provision. This passage contradicts our view of pride in major ways by illuminating the truth that God lifts up the humble while scattering those who are proud, even in their innermost thoughts alone.

What a challenge!

No one wants to admit to pride. But, don't we all wrestle with it? Don't we often chase reactions from those around us—adoration from the world—rather than searching for and centering on the heart and will of our Father?

The Christmas story itself is filled with illustrations of humility, from Mary's song, to the arrival of Jesus Christ himself in a lowly, dirty manger.

Our savior did not arrive decked in finery, ready to impress. So, why do we live our lives like we deserve better?

Today, draw near to God by asking him to point out sources of pride and actions based on pride in your life. Ask him to transform you, giving you a humble heart that reflects his might and provision alone.

Journal

What are the barriers to humility in your life? When you self-reflect and ask God to reveal thoughts and actions that are designed to elevate yourself, what do you find? Ask God to help break down these barriers while allowing you to trust in him and better reflect humility to those around you.

Listen:
The Intention vs. the Challenge

Even a fool who keeps silent is considered wise; when he closes his lips, he is deemed intelligent.

Proverbs 17:28

Be still before the LORD and wait patiently for him; fret not yourself over the one who prospers in his way, over the man who carries out evil devices!

Psalm 37:7

Seek the LORD and his strength; seek his presence continually!

1 Chronicles 16:11

But he [Jesus] would withdraw to desolate places and pray.

Luke 5:16

Call to me and I will answer you, and will tell you great and hidden things that you have not known.

Jeremiah 33:3

Behold, I stand at the door and knock. If anyone hears my voice and opens the door, I will come in to him and eat with him, and he with me.

Revelation 3:20

WHAT DOES YOUR TIME WITH GOD LOOK LIKE?
I know what you picture when you think of diving into scripture and devotion (at least what I picture!), but, what's the reality? Are you alone, free of all distractions, with time and space to just listen? Or, do you throw on a podcast or worship music in the car and try to focus on his glory, promising that tomorrow will be better?

I'm not downing our car worship sessions or podcasts. But, when they become our foundation, we miss out on something critical: we forget to *listen* to God.

So far, we've focused on seeking quietness and finding shelter in our God, dwelling in him. Today, let's go even more basic (but perhaps more central). Let's listen.

I'll keep this short; I want you to be able to start today!

Think in terms of earthly relationships: when someone is *really* listening, we feel more able to express what's important to us. Likewise, when we listen—without thinking of other tasks or our next words—we pick up on things that we would have otherwise missed.

Listening to God takes patience, practice and discipline. It requires a willingness to change our current routines and might even feel uncomfortable; that doesn't make it less crucial.

Scripture makes it clear that some of the most valuable time with God starts with quiet. Even Jesus was known for retreating to solitude to listen to God and pray. Our times of worship and praise, especially on the go, allow us to pray and sing to him, but they don't allow us to listen.

Listening can't be devalued. Scriptures, like those today, make it clear that God will speak to and move through those who listen to him. Maybe that's because listening requires true devotion, it requires an open, willing heart that, as mentioned before, can be unnatural for us.

For us to truly prepare for this Advent season, to draw near to him in every sense, we must search for God's voice. Whether that's a sense of peace, a gentle leading in our hearts, a conviction that we must change or repent, or Old-

Testament-style conversation, God *will* speak if we are willing to listen.

Are you willing to start today?

Journal

Keep it simple. Spend ten minutes in a quiet space, asking God to draw near to your heart, then, listen. Commit to this daily and journal what comes to mind at the conclusion of each attempt.

Remain Faithful when Impulse Reigns Supreme

You shall be careful therefore to do as the LORD your God has commanded you. You shall not turn aside to the right hand or to the left. You shall walk in all the way that the LORD your God has commanded you, that you may live, and that it may go well with you, and that you may live long in the land that you shall possess.

Deuteronomy 5:32–33

And now, Israel, what does the LORD your God require of you but to fear the LORD your God, to walk in all his ways, to love him, to serve the LORD your God with all your heart and with all your soul, and to keep the commandments and statutes of the LORD, which I am commanding you today for your good?

Deuteronomy 10:12–13

Know therefore that the LORD your God, the faithful God who keeps covenant and steadfast love with those who love him and keep his commandments, to a thousand generations, and repays to their face those who hate him, by destroying them. He will not be slack with one who hates him. He will repay him to his face.

Deuteronomy 7:9–10

Only fear the LORD and serve him faithfully with all your heart.
For consider what great things he has done for you.

1 Samuel 12:24

The saying is trustworthy, for: If we have died with him, we will
also live with him; if we endure, we will also reign with him; if
we deny him, he also will deny us; if we are faithless, he remains
faithful—for he cannot deny himself.

2 Timothy 2:11–13

FAITHFULNESS HAS BECOME SOMEWHAT SUBJECTIVE IN OUR culture. We set about on big tasks and journeys with the best of intentions and great determination, but we find ourselves off task or on a "new" and "better" journey before we know it.

We decide to lose weight and get in shape. It becomes hard or we face a setback, so, we decide to call it off, or, give ourselves time to rest before recommitting, settling for less than our original goal.

We jump into marriage, but real life hits. It's hard. We decide to find happiness elsewhere.

We make promises to others. Life happens. We apologize and explain why the circumstances holding us back are just "out of our control."

In our human state, follow-through is difficult. We've become creatures of impulse, willing and able to settle for less than we intended, even if that original intention was part of God's design for our lives. We've become pretty excellent at explaining to ourselves and others why falling short is okay; we even believe it.

Our worldly notion of impulse and temporary gratification could not be in greater contrast to our Father's plan, vision and his entire being.

When we read about God's faithfulness in the Bible, it should shock us. We learn that he keeps his covenants to the thousandth generation, that he is unwavering and steady in his commitments. We learn that it is this picture of steadfast faithfulness that should inspire our faith and trust in him.

We also learn that this, and nothing less, should be our own model when it comes to making commitments. We should serve with this level of faithfulness, even when it contradicts our own notions and earthly examples of commitment. We learn that faithfulness to our God and his calling during this life will be rewarded in eternity.

We aren't trained to think in these terms, in the light of eternity. It would make many of the "good" things in this life seem meaningless. It would make us look different. It would *change* us.

Maybe that's what we're missing.

This season makes it even more evident. God's sending of his son, his perfect son, sent to our sinful world to be faced with the same trials and temptations we face, yet, to overcome them, was a result of God's generational, eternal faithfulness, so intricate and everlasting that we often fail—or feel unable—to grasp it. It is *that* different from even the best examples we have to follow during our time in this world.

Maybe that's why it's so important. This difference based on scriptural promises is what requires our attention during this time of Advent.

By considering God's faithfulness, in the Bible and in our own lives, while trying to modify the way we handle commitments to others and our faithfulness to God, we can draw nearer to him, more fully experiencing the fulfillment of his promise both during Advent and beyond.

Journal

What impulses block you from fully trusting in God's plan for your life? In what way has he demonstrated his love and faithfulness toward you? How does this change the way you see him and your overall relationship with him?

Accept True Gifts:
#Blessed

"Blessed are the poor in spirit, for theirs is the kingdom of heaven. Blessed are those who mourn, for they shall be comforted. Blessed are the meek, for they shall inherit the earth. Blessed are those who hunger and thirst for righteousness, for they shall be satisfied. Blessed are the merciful, for they shall receive mercy. Blessed are the pure in heart, for they shall see God. Blessed are the peacemakers, for they shall be called sons of God. Blessed are those who are persecuted for righteousness sake, for theirs is the kingdom of heaven. Blessed are you when others revile you and persecute you and utter all kinds of evil against you falsely on my account. Rejoice and be glad, for your reward is great in heaven, for so they persecuted the prophets who were before you."

Matthew 5:3–12

But the fruit of the Spirit is love, joy, peace, patience, kindness, goodness, faithfulness, gentleness, self-control: against such things there is no law. And those who belong to Christ Jesus have crucified the flesh with its passions and desires. If we live by the Spirit, let us also keep in step with the Spirit.

Galatians 5:22–25

WE LIVE IN A WORLD OF COMPARISON. We could spend all day arguing whether social media is a blessing or a curse (we discussed this a bit on day 21) but, one thing is certain: it's never been easier to see inside the lives of others.

The problem with this is that when we, and others, share the minute details of our lives, we tend to put our best foot forward. Who wants to stare at others barely hanging on, sitting at a desk and passing out on the couch by 8pm?

One especially prevalent trend this habit of ours has produced goes by a simple term: #blessed. Someone scores a sweet corner office promotion? #blessed. Someone else has time for a third cup of especially expensive coffee on their day off? #blessed. Someone's kids fall asleep without a fight during naptime, giving them an extra 20 minutes to read in silence? #blessed.

It's all innocent and well-intentioned... it doesn't hurt anyone... or does it?

How about friends who've been out of work for months? Those wondering how to cover their next grocery trip? Those longing for kids—whether they nap or not?

I'd like to argue that our trend of highlighting our blessings might be the most modern way to one-up one another... and I'm just as guilty as you.

To understand God's view of blessings, we have to look beyond that starry manger scene, toward what that first arrival of our King facilitated: the truest form of blessing.

In today's scripture passage, Christ makes it clear who the blessed are... and they don't fall into our standard, Insta-based definition. The weak. The meek. The pure in heart. The peacemakers.

Let that sink in.

Later, in Galatians, we have another reveal. We learn about the fruits of the Spirit... about blessings in action: Love. Joy. Kindness. Goodness.

You see, we *are* blessed. We might have unlimited clothing budgets and new cars. Or, we might hide the Christmas toy catalogs to avoid having to disappoint our kids with a "less-than" quantity of gifts Christmas morning. But, these definitions mean nothing to our Father.

He looks for those who seek him with their whole hearts. He looks for those who look past what the world deems "worthy," who accept and acknowledge his blessings.

Don't get me wrong, there are things to celebrate in this life. God can (and does) bless us in other ways. But, we must be careful in examining our own motivations and standards.

What if we could align our desires with the blessings God has in store for us? Those he promises and holds out for us in an unlimited supply, waiting for us to recognize them and utilize them for his purposes? I'm willing to wager the results would be truly life-altering.

Journal

How can you seek God's heart this Advent season? In what ways has God truly blessed you, according to those blessings listed in today's scriptures? How can you use these true gifts to bless others?

Dwell on the Glory: Adore Him

In those days a decree went out from Caesar Augustus that all the world should be registered. This was the first registration when Quirinius was governor of Syria. And all went to be registered, each to his own town. And Joseph also went up from Galilee, from the town of Nazareth, to Judea, to the city of David, which is called Bethlehem, because he was of the house and lineage of David, to be registered with Mary, his betrothed, who was with child. And while they were there, the time came for her to give birth. And she gave birth to her firstborn son and wrapped him in swaddling cloths and laid him in a manger, because there was no place for them in the inn.

And in the same region there were shepherds out in the field, keeping watch over their flock by night. And an angel of the Lord appeared to them, and the glory of the Lord shone around them, and they were filled with great fear. And the angel said to them, "Fear not, for behold, I bring you good news of great joy that will be for all the people. For unto you is born this day in the city of David a Savior, who is Christ the Lord. And this will be a sign for you: you will find a baby wrapped in swaddling cloths and lying in a manger." And suddenly there was with the angel a multitude of the heavenly host praising God and saying,

"Glory to God in the highest,
  and on earth peace among those with whom he is
pleased!"

When the angels went away from them into heaven, the shepherds said to one another, "Let us go over to Bethlehem and see this thing that has happened, which the Lord has made known to us." And they went with haste and found Mary and Joseph, and the baby lying in a manger. And when they saw it, they made known the saying that had been told them concerning this child. And all who heard it wondered at what the shepherds told them. But Mary treasured up all these things, pondering them in her heart. And the shepherds returned, glorifying and praising God for all they had heard and seen, as it had been told them.

Luke 2:1–20

I T'S EASY TO SKIM THROUGH THE CHRISTMAS STORY, isn't it? We've heard it, seen it, reenacted it and read it hundreds of times. Yes, Jesus's birth is the reason for the season, but, sometimes we still—unwillingly—take the story for granted.

Let's change that. Today, before the holiday traditions take over, spend a little more time with the passage above. Imagine yourself in that stable. Dwell on the glory of it all.

Interestingly, the idea of glory has a lot to do with the Christmas story, especially as told in the book of Luke. Writing in Greek, to the Gentiles, Luke uses forms of glory—or "doxa"—three times in the passage above, 13 times in his complete Gospel.

A lot of times, we consider glory to be an action, something we give to God (which we should). In always thinking this way, we forget that glory is an intrinsic attribute of God. Glory is splendor, brightness, magnificence, excellence. God. Is. Glory.

When we "give God glory," we recognize what only he can be, what he *is.*

The Christmas story illustrates this perfectly, as such, we should take the time to dwell on it.

God out of his perfect knowledge and love for us, sent his perfect son to us. Foretold by prophets, pronounced by angels and revealed to shepherds and beyond, our Savior came, in all his glory—his alone—to bridge the gap between God and man... between God and us.

We may not have been present that night, but, we can still dwell on the glory of it all. We can marvel over the coming of the Christ child. We can and should adore him, today and always.

Glory to God, glory in the highest. Let us draw near to him. Let us adore him.

"O Come Let Us Adore Him"
John Francis Wade

O come, all ye faithful,
Joyful and triumphant,
O come ye, O come ye to Bethlehem.
Come and behold Him,
Born the King of Angels!

O come, let us adore Him,
O come, let us adore Him,
O come, let us adore Him,
Christ the Lord.

Sing, alleluia,
All ye choirs of angels;
O sing, all ye blissful ones of heav'n above.
Glory to God
In the highest glory!

O come, let us adore Him,
O come, let us adore Him,

O come, let us adore Him,
Christ the Lord.

Yea, Lord, we greet Thee,
Born this happy morning;
Jesus, to Thee be the glory giv'n;
Word of the Father,
Now in flesh appearing,

O come, let us adore Him,
O come, let us adore Him,
O come, let us adore Him,
Christ the Lord

Journal

What does God's glory mean to you? What part of the Christmas story stands out to you today? Write a prayer to God, thanking him for sending his son. Take the time to adore him.

Notes & Acknowledgements

FIRST OF ALL—thank you.

Thank you for following along with me this Advent season.

Thank you for being patient with my first published devotional.

Thank you for being willing to look at this season differently.

I hope this devotional challenged you—I know it challenged my heart and helped me grow during the research and writing process. I talk a lot about this world, and this life, but, I do it because I so often fall into the routines of this world, taking comfort in all the wrong things and letting other things feel bigger than me, forgetting that nothing is bigger than my Savior and his love for me, for all of us.

All scriptures were taken from the English Standard Version translation of the Bible, a version that employs an "essentially literal" translation philosophy, unless otherwise noted. Spacing was adjusted occasionally for devotional reading purposes.

Thank you to my husband, who challenged me during the writing process to continue when I was falling behind, and who gave me the leeway to focus fully (which is not always easy with 5 kids roaming our home!). Without his support, thoughts on the final product and loving prompts, this project would not have come together.

Thank you to my kids, patient enough to let mommy type "her book!" I often took up your space, and television time to get through!

Thank you to Benjamin Vrbicek for creating the interior design and layout of *Draw Near*. This is no small task, and I am grateful.

In Proverbs, we're told that iron sharpens iron. This is so true, and vital to the Christian walk. For those who've served this role in my life, I am so very grateful.

Thank you to those who have challenged me at various points in my walk with Christ to seek him first, to acknowledge my shortcomings and to learn. I have grown because of you. This list could go on forever, but if you've served as a Sunday School teacher, a youth leader, a college mentor, a pastor, a small group member, a Christian friend willing to dive deep into tough conversations or any other number of roles in my life, I've learned from you and I am grateful for your heart.

Most importantly, thank you to my personal Savior, the one I've needed to turn back around to on so many occasions, but who has always been waiting, arms wide open, full of grace and forgiveness that is so far from my understanding. Thank you for drawing near to me, for drawing me closer to you, your truth and your presence, regardless of the situations of this life. Thank you for paying my debt and giving grace so freely.

If you've read this book because you know me (thank you for your support!) or because a friend or acquaintance urged you to do so, but, you don't have a relationship with Christ, or, are wondering what all of this is really all about, I would like to challenge you to go deeper. Open your heart and dive into God's word. Ask him to reveal himself to you. Ask it over and over again. Speak to that friend or to a known Christian in your life. Visit a local church. Ask questions. Share your doubts. Let yourself be known. God is waiting for you to draw near to him with his arms wide, wide open. He is good and he is always there. Trust in that as you pursue his truth.

Before the mountains were brought forth,
or ever you had formed the earth and the world,
from everlasting to everlasting you are God.

Psalm 90:2

Read more of Laura's writing at
www.TakeTwoBlog.com.

Made in the USA
Coppell, TX
20 April 2021